# Dinosaurs
## Preschool Basics Activity Workbook

## This book belongs to:

_____

_____

Copyright © 2019 by KIDSFUN

All rights reserved. No part of this publication may be reproduced, distributed, or transmitted in any form or by any means, including photocopying, recording, or other electronic or mechanical methods, without the prior written permission of the publisher, except in the case of brief quotations embodied in critical reviews and certain other non-commercial uses permitted by copyright law.

# Table of Contents

Number Tracing.

Match the Number.

Let's Count!

What a Difference.

More or Less?

Big vs. Small.

Compare sizes.

Shape.

The picture that comes next!

Number Fun.

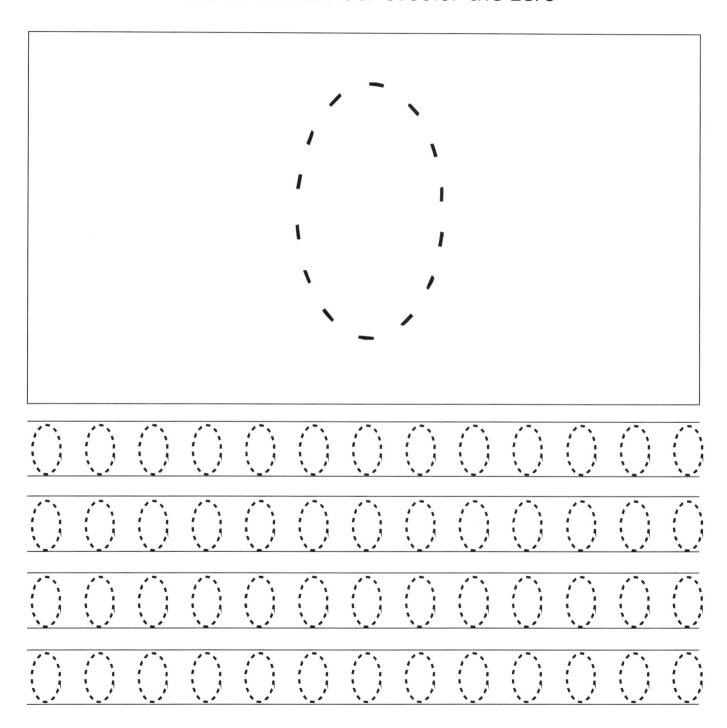

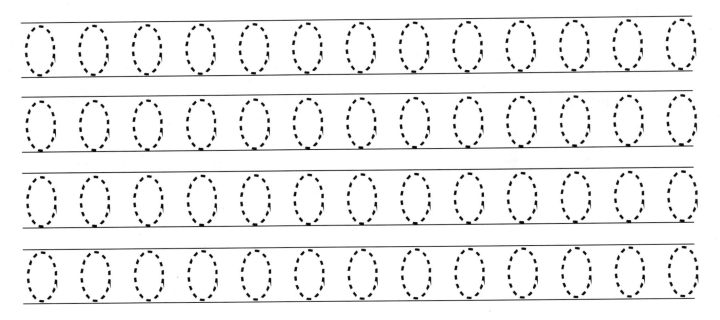

## Circle the square with _O_ image.

## Color _O_ Dinosaur.

# 1 One

Trace the number and color picture.

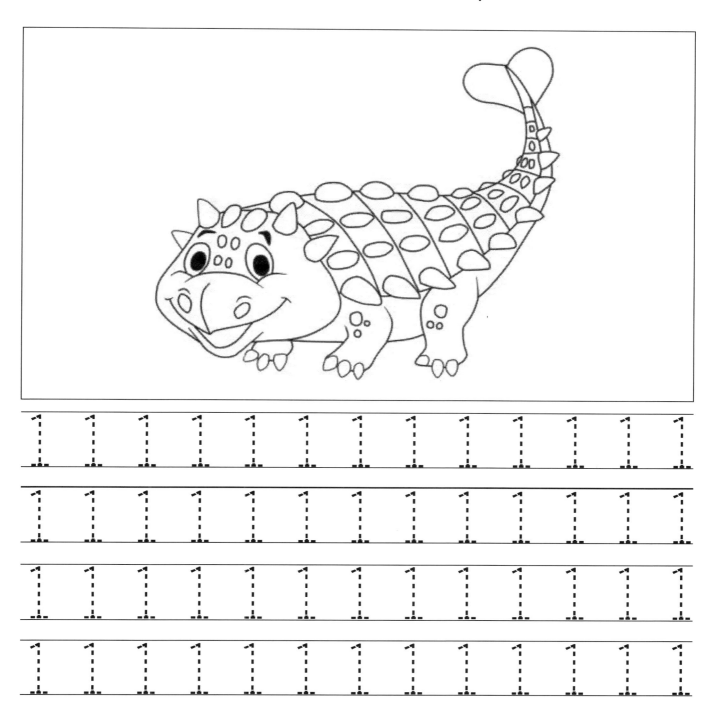

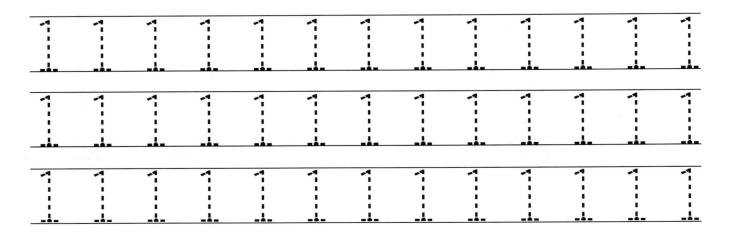

## Circle the square with _1_ image.

 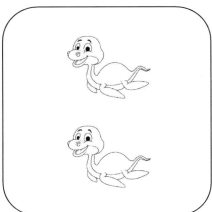 

## Color _1_ Dinosaur.

# 2 Two

Trace the number and color them.

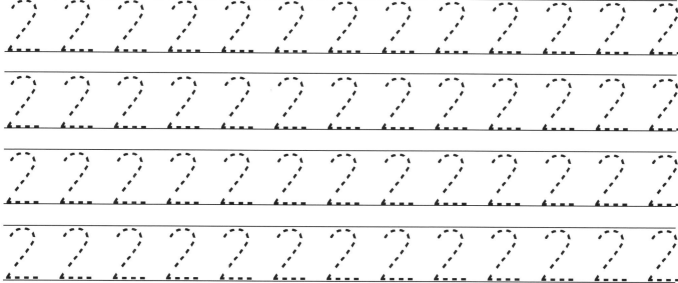

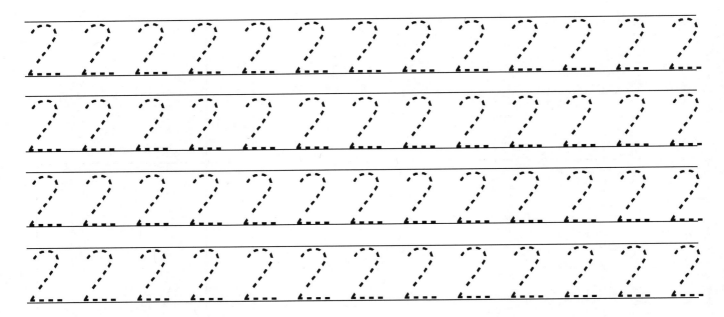

## Circle the square with <u>2</u> image.

## Color <u>2</u> Dinosaur.

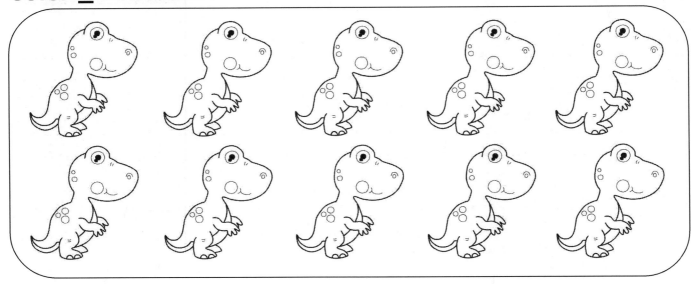

# 3 Three

Trace the number and color them.

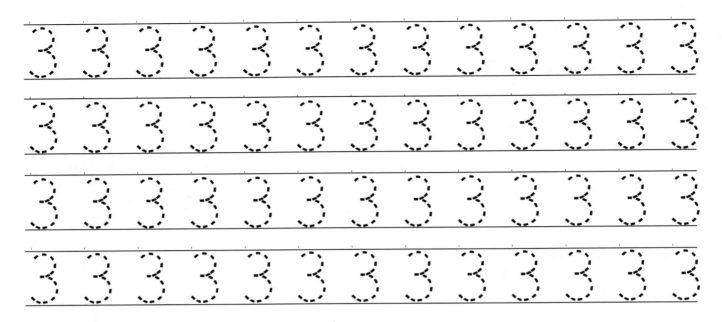

## Circle the square with 3 image.

## Color 3 Dinosaur.

# 4 Four

Trace the number and color them.

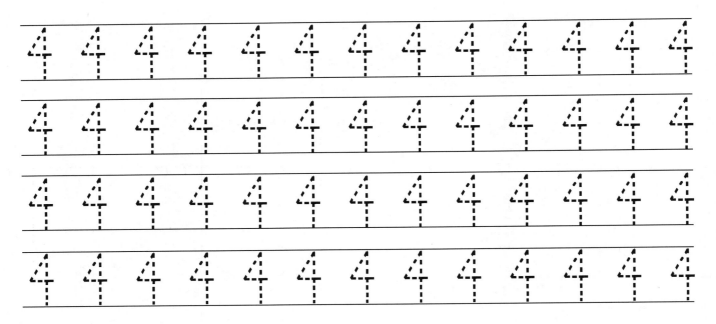

## Circle the square with <u>4</u> image.

## Color <u>4</u> Dinosaur.

# 5 Five

Trace the number and color them.

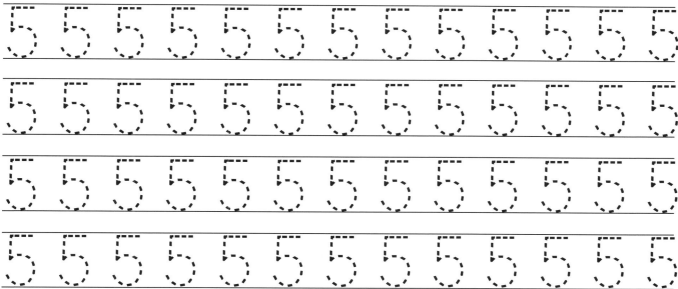

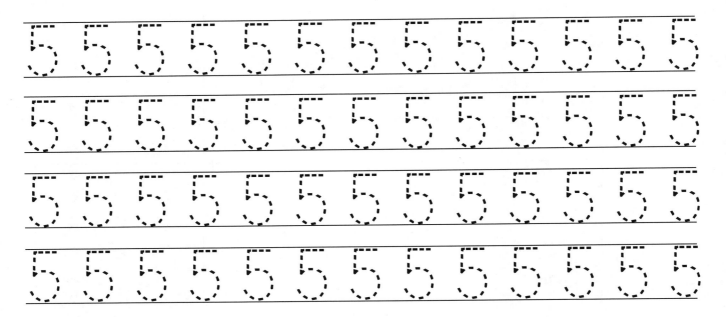

## Circle the square with <u>5</u> image.

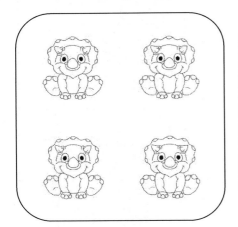  

## Color <u>5</u> Dinosaur.

# 6 Six

Trace the number and color them.

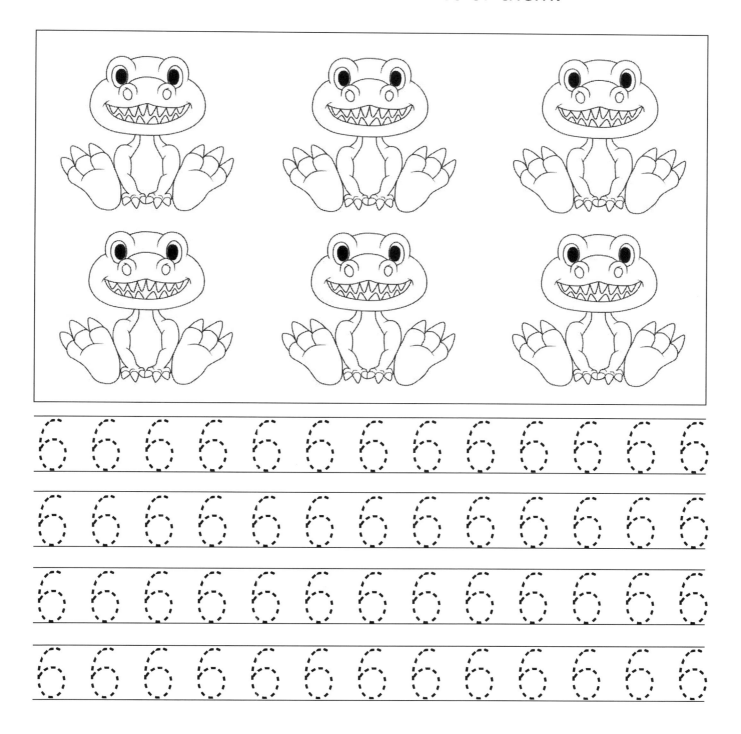

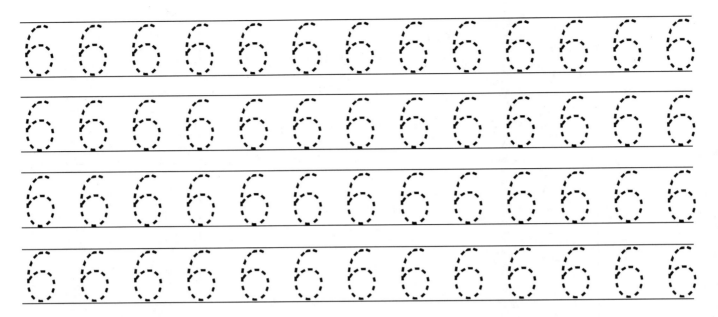

## Circle the square with <u>6</u> image.

## Color <u>6</u> Dinosaur.

# 7 Seven

Trace the number and color them.

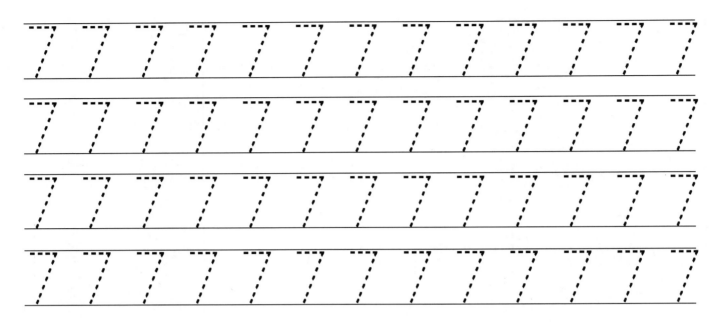

## Circle the square with Z image.

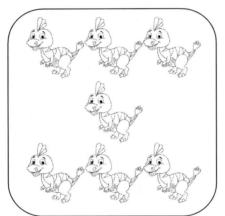 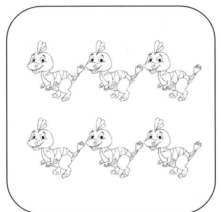 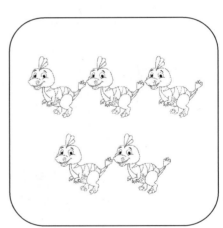

## Color Z Dinosaur.

# 8 Eight
Trace the number and color them.

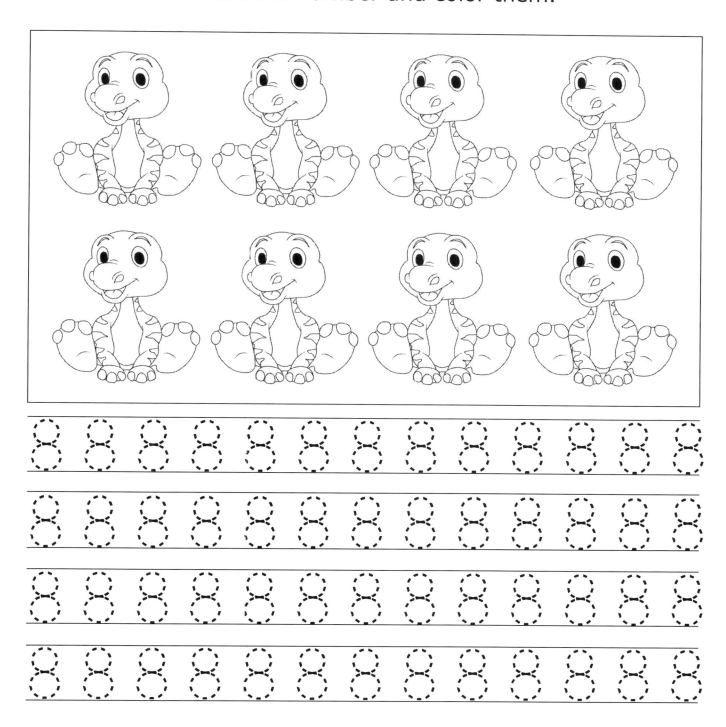

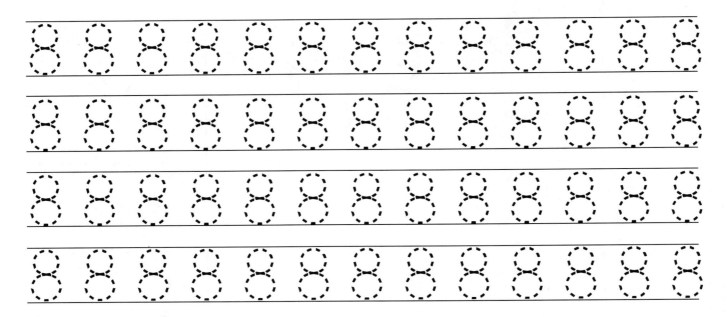

## Circle the square with *8* image.

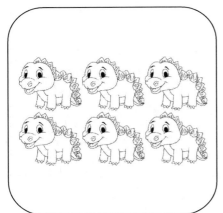  

## Color *8* Dinosaur.

Trace the number and color them.

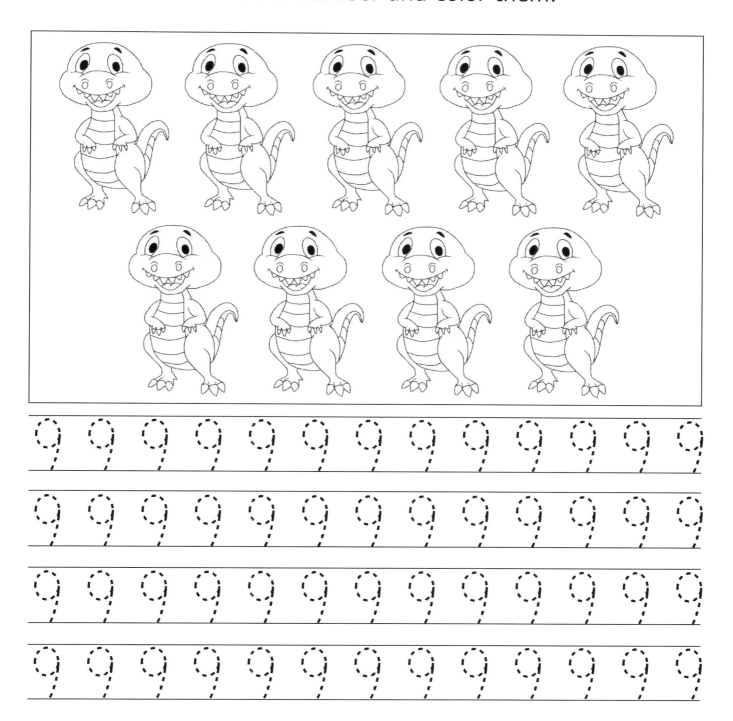

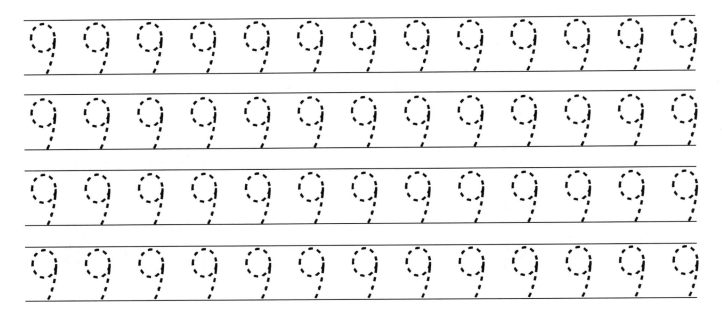

## Circle the square with <u>9</u> image.

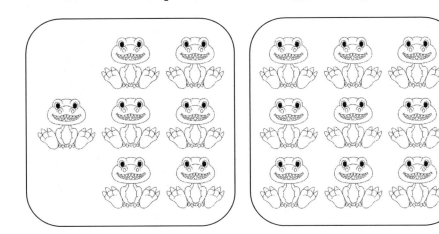 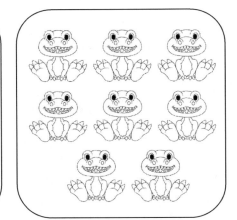

## Color <u>9</u> Dinosaur.

# 10 Ten

Trace the number and color them.

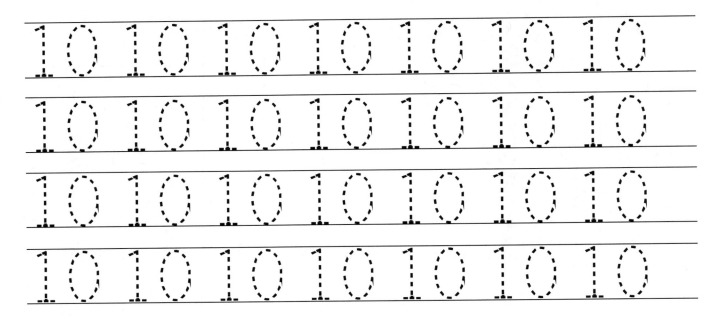

## Circle the square with _10_ image.

 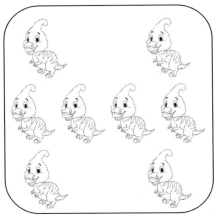 

## Color _10_ Dinosaur.

## Color the Dinosaurs and Match the Number!

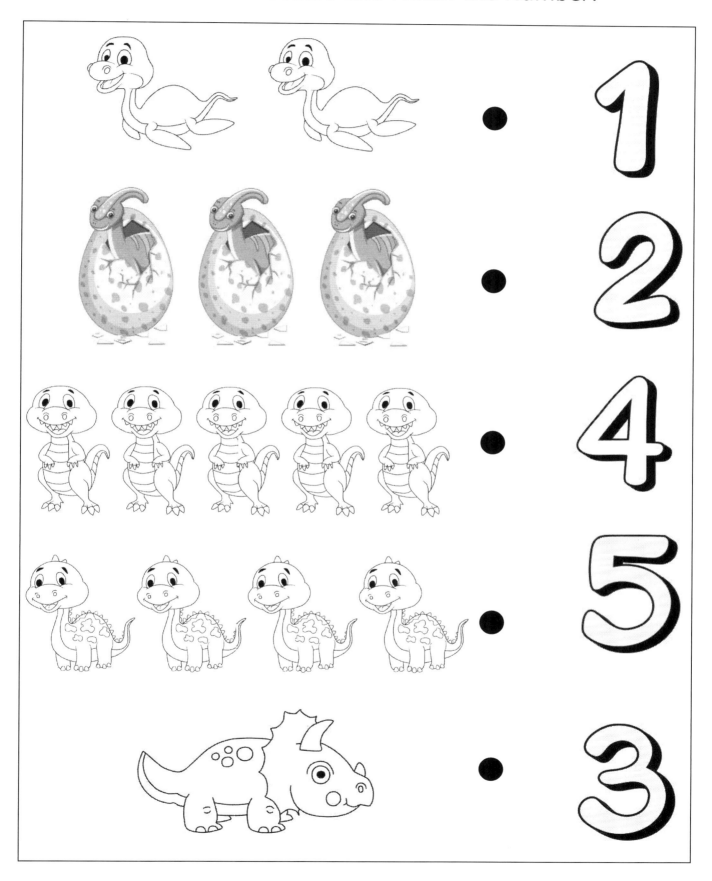

# Color the Dinosaurs and Match the Number!

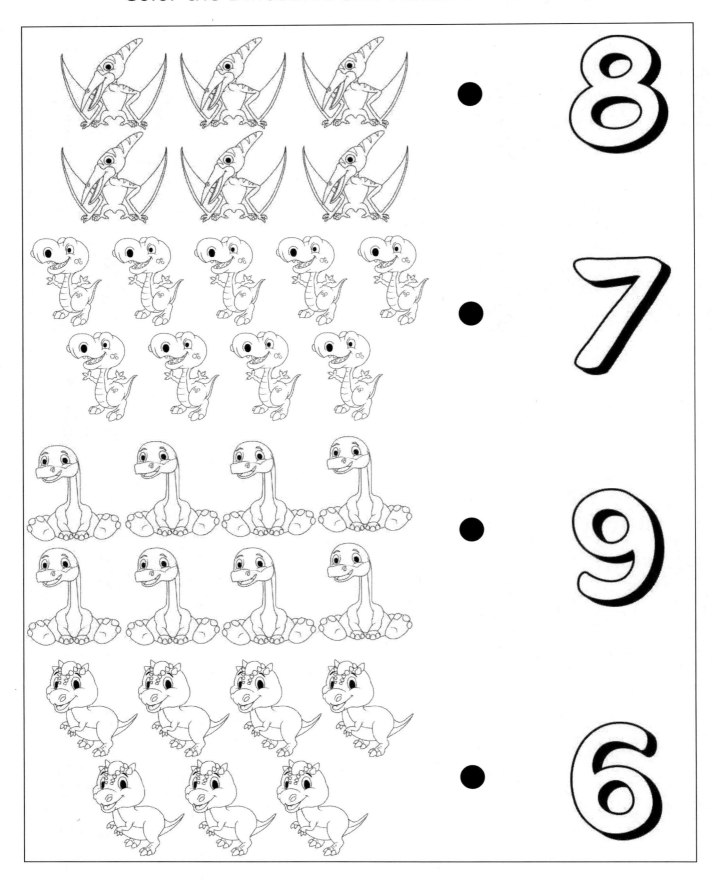

# Let's Count!
Count each Dinosaurs and fill your answers in below.

How many 🦕 ? _____

How many 🦕 ? _____

How many 🦕 ? _____

# Let's Count!
Count each kind of Dinosaurs and fill your answers in below.

How many  ? _____

How many  ? _____

How many  ? _____

# Let's Count!
Count each kind of Dinosaurs and fill your answers in below.

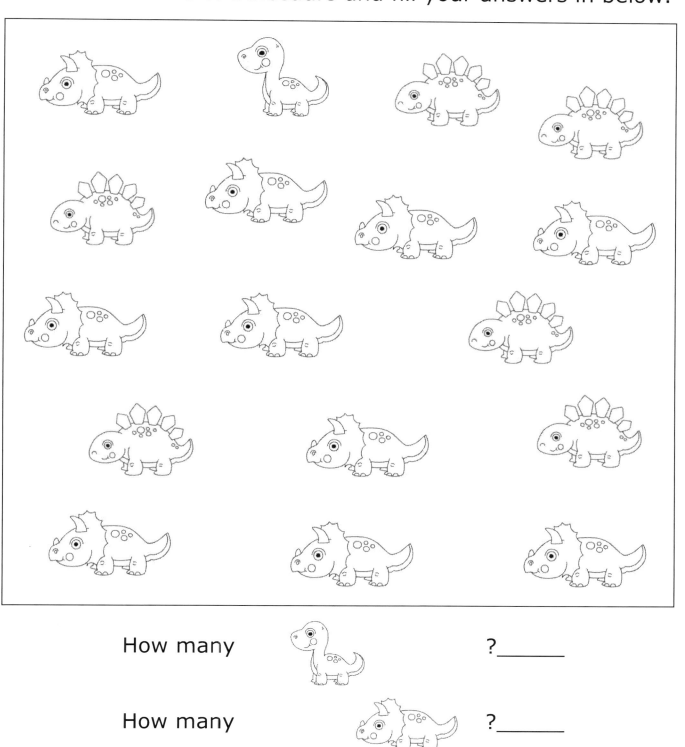

How many 🦕 ?_____

How many 🦕 ?_____

How many 🦕 ?_____

# Let's Count!
Count each kind of Dinosaurs and fill your answers in below.

How many ![dino1] ?_____

How many ![dino2] ?_____

# What a Difference
Look at the pictures below and color the correct picture.

# What a Difference
Look at the pictures below and color the correct picture.

# What a Difference
Color in the pictures. Make them all different!

# What a Difference
Color in the pictures. Make them all different!

# More or Less?

Look at the pictures in each box and circle the group that has **more.**

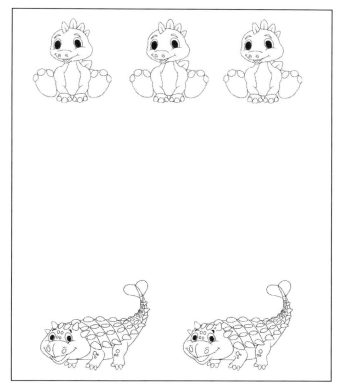

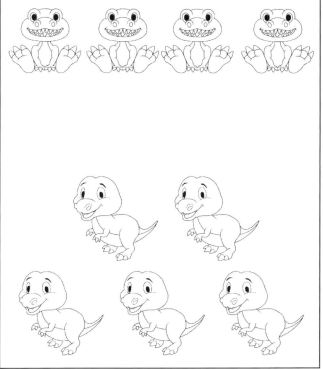

# More or Less?

Look at the pictures in each box and circle the group that has **less**.

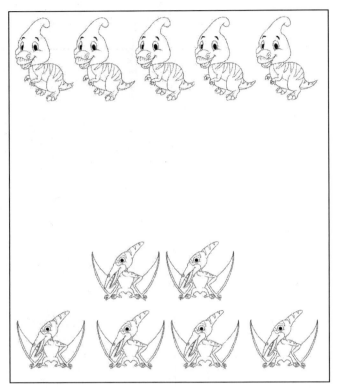

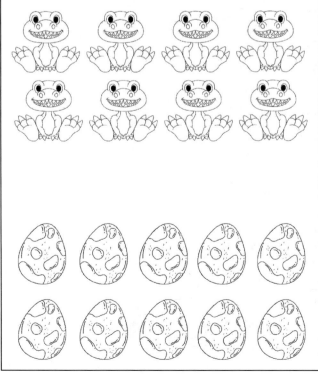

# More or Less?

Count the number of images and write the total number in each box. Circle the box with **more** images in each row.

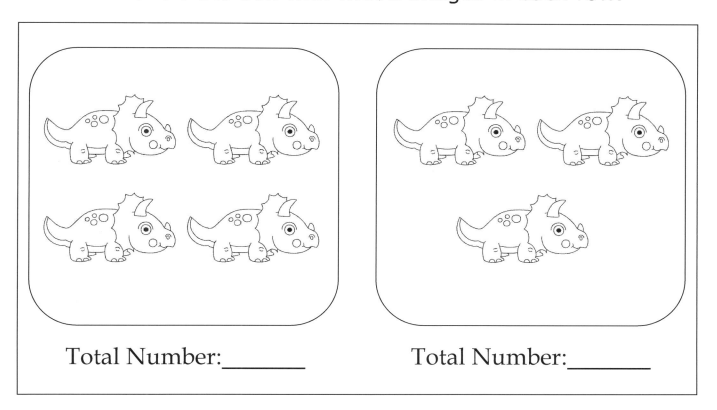

Total Number:_____     Total Number:_____

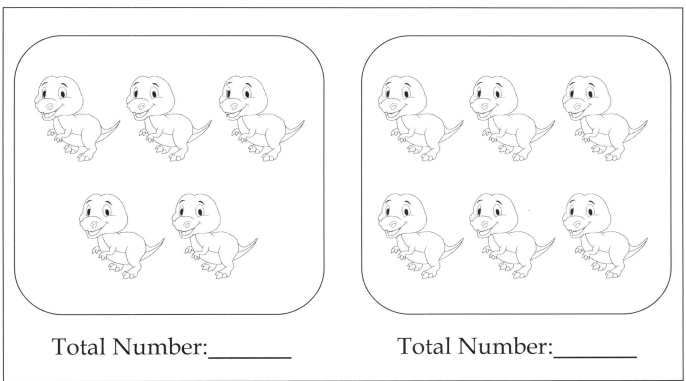

Total Number:_____     Total Number:_____

# More or Less?

Count the number of images and write the total number in each box. Circle the box with **less** images in each row.

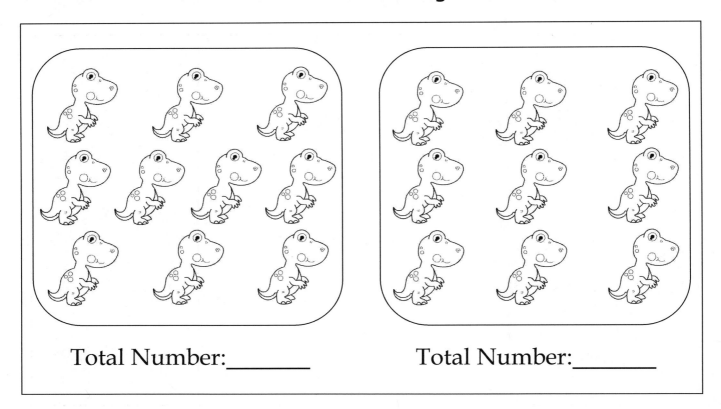

Total Number:_____   Total Number:_____

Total Number:_____   Total Number:_____

# Big vs. Small

Look at the picture below and answer the question by circling the correct picture.

Which is **bigger?**

Which is **smaller?**

Which is **smaller?**

Which is **bigger?**

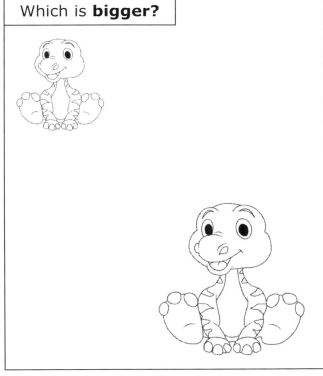

# Big vs. Small

Look at the picture below and answer the question by circling the correct picture.

| Which is **bigger?** | Which is **smaller?** |
|---|---|
|  | 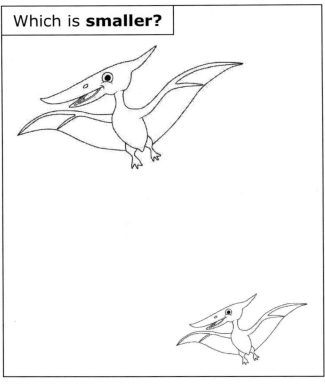 |
| Which is **smaller?** | Which is **bigger?** |
|  |  |

# Big vs. Small

Look at the picture below and answer the question by drawing the correct picture.

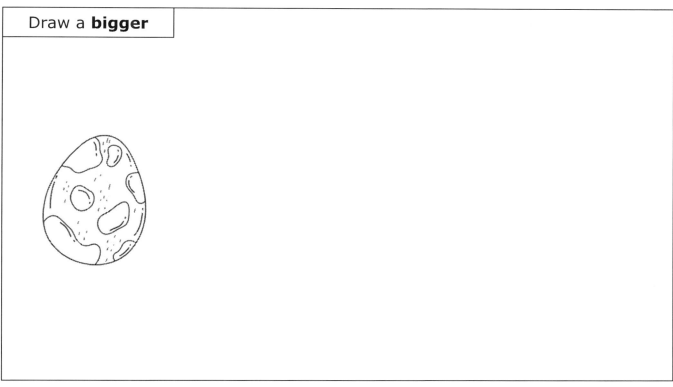

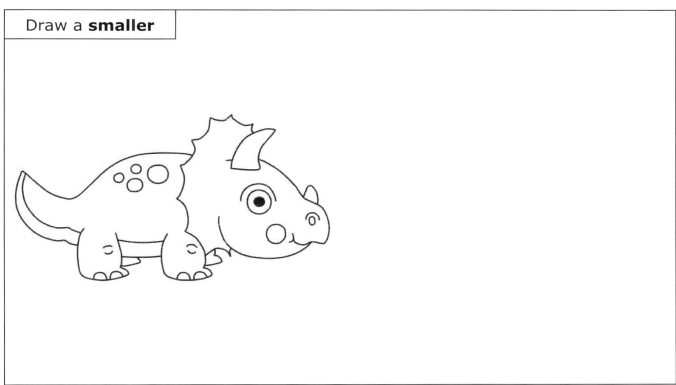

# Big vs. Small

Look at the picture below and answer the question by drawing the correct picture.

Draw a **bigger**

Draw a **smaller**

# Big vs. Small

Look at the picture below and answer the question by drawing the correct picture.

Draw a **bigger**

Draw a **smaller**

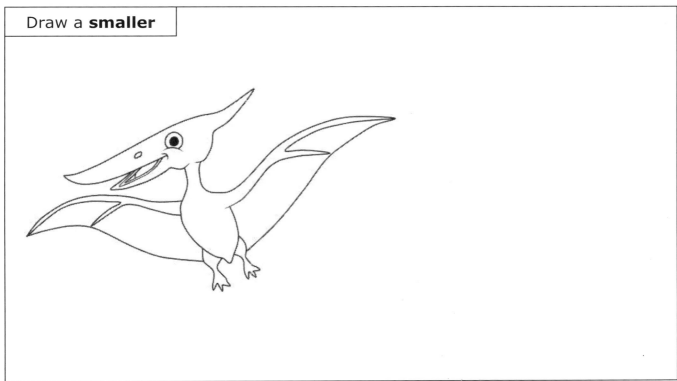

# Big vs. Small

Look at the picture below and answer the question by drawing the correct picture.

Draw a **bigger**

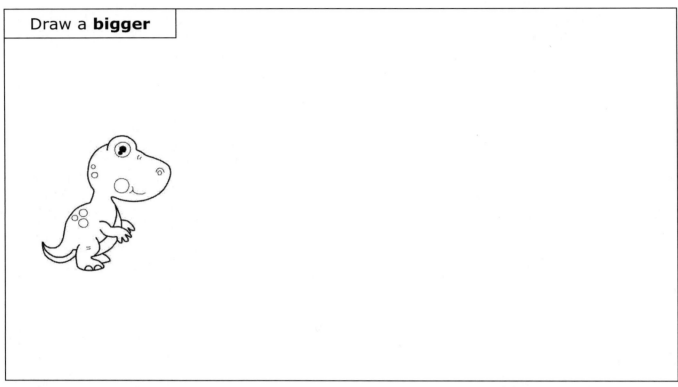

Draw a **smaller**

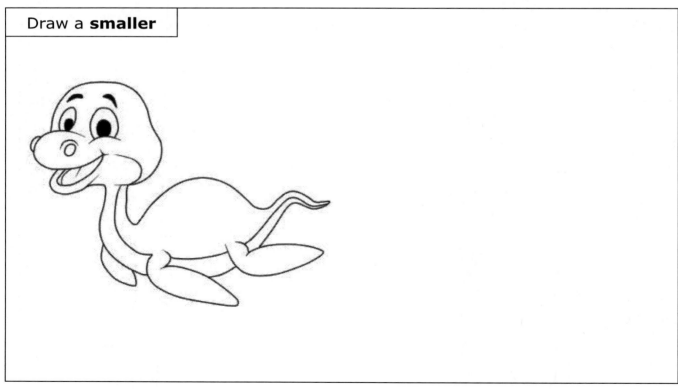

# Compare sizes

Small     Medium     Large

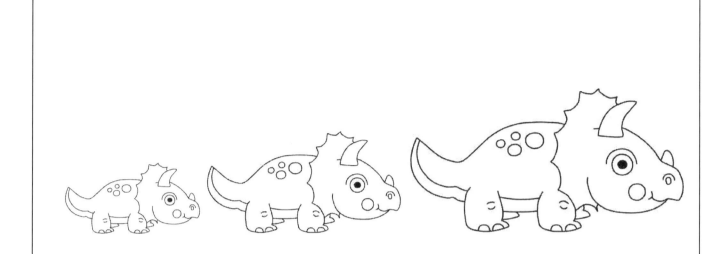

Color the large in red, medium in yellow and small in green

Color the large in red, medium in yellow and small in green

# Compare sizes
## Color the large in red, medium in yellow and small in green

## Color the large in red, medium in yellow and small in green

# Shape - Circle

**circle**

Let's trace the circle!

Let's draw the circle!

A circle has _____ sides and _____ corners.

Circles are hiding in the images. Find and color the circles!

# Shape – Triangle

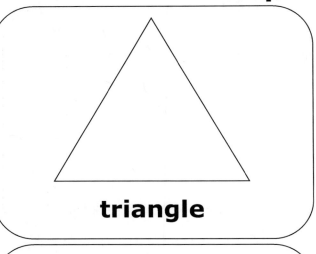

triangle

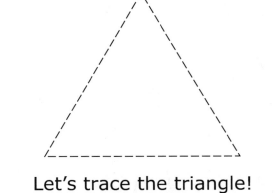

Let's trace the triangle!

Let's draw the triangle!

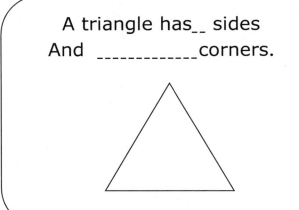

A triangle has __ sides
And _____ corners.

Triangle are hiding in the images. Find and color the

# Shape – Rectangle

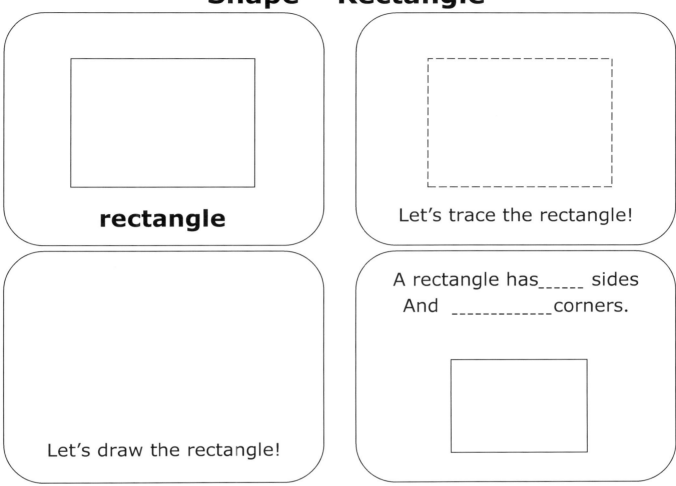

Rectangle are hiding in the images. Find and color the rectangle!

# Shape – Square

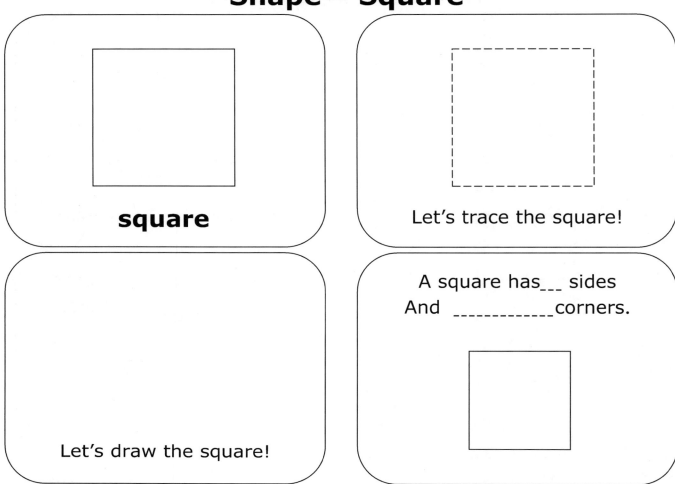

**square**

Let's trace the square!

Let's draw the square!

A square has ___ sides
And _____ corners.

Square are hiding in the images. Find and color the square!

# Shape – Trapezoid

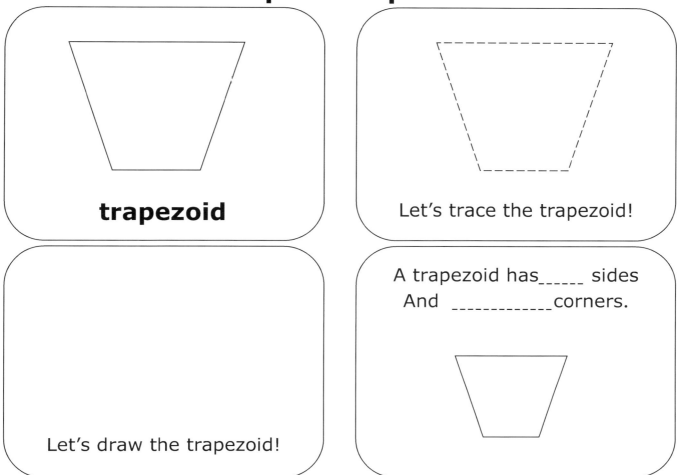

**trapezoid**

Let's trace the trapezoid!

Let's draw the trapezoid!

A trapezoid has _____ sides And _____ corners.

Trapezoid are hiding in the images. Find and color the trapezoid!

# Shape – Pentagon

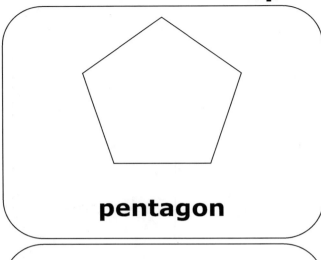

**pentagon**

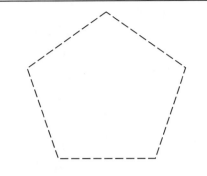

Let's trace the pentagon!

Let's draw the pentagon!

A pentagon has _____ sides
And _____ corners.

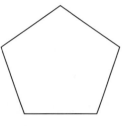

Pentagon are hiding in the images. Find and color the pentagon!

# Shape – Hexagon

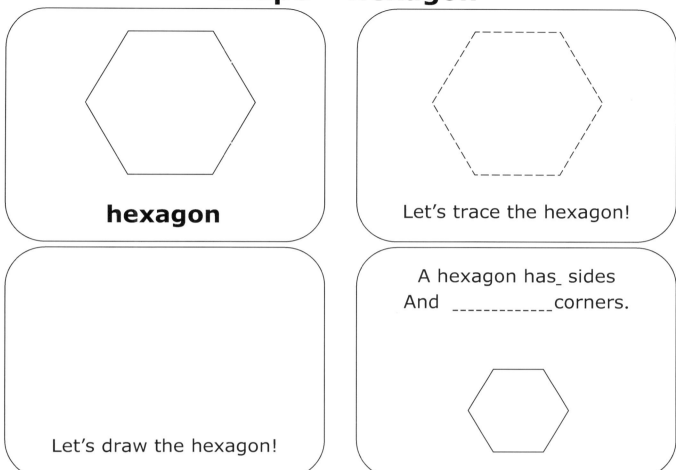

Let's trace the hexagon!

Let's draw the hexagon!

A hexagon has_ sides
And _____ corners.

Hexagon are hiding in the images. Find and color the hexagon!

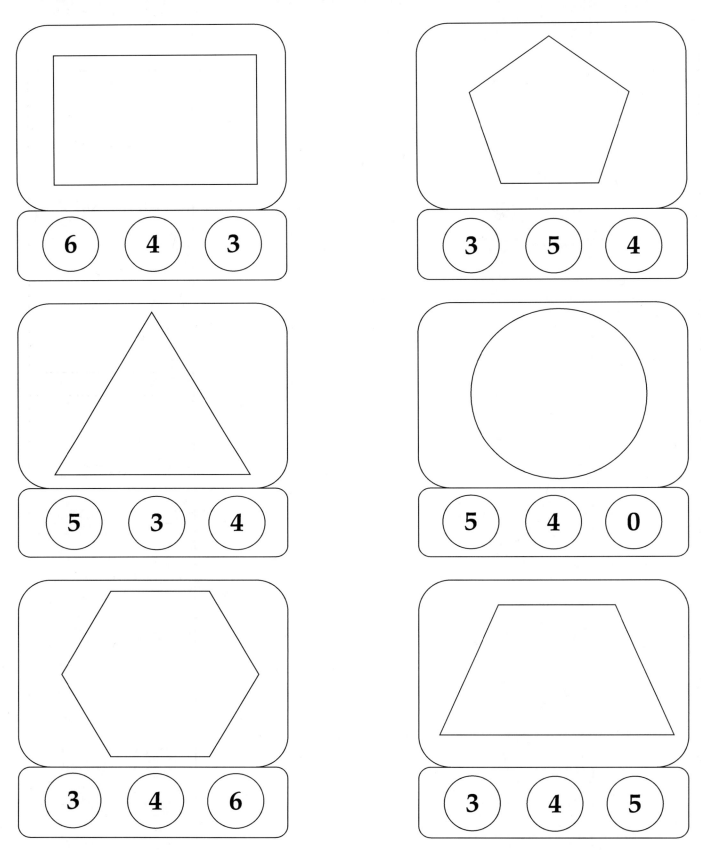

# The picture that comes next!

Look at the patterns below. Cut out the images and paste the image that comes last in each box.

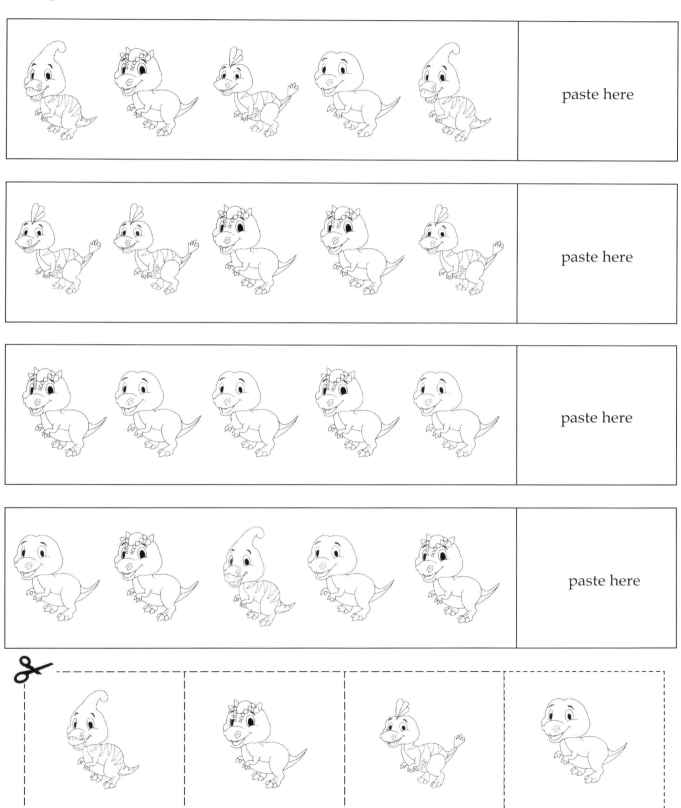

# The picture that comes next!

Look at the patterns below. Cut out the images and paste the image that comes last in each box.

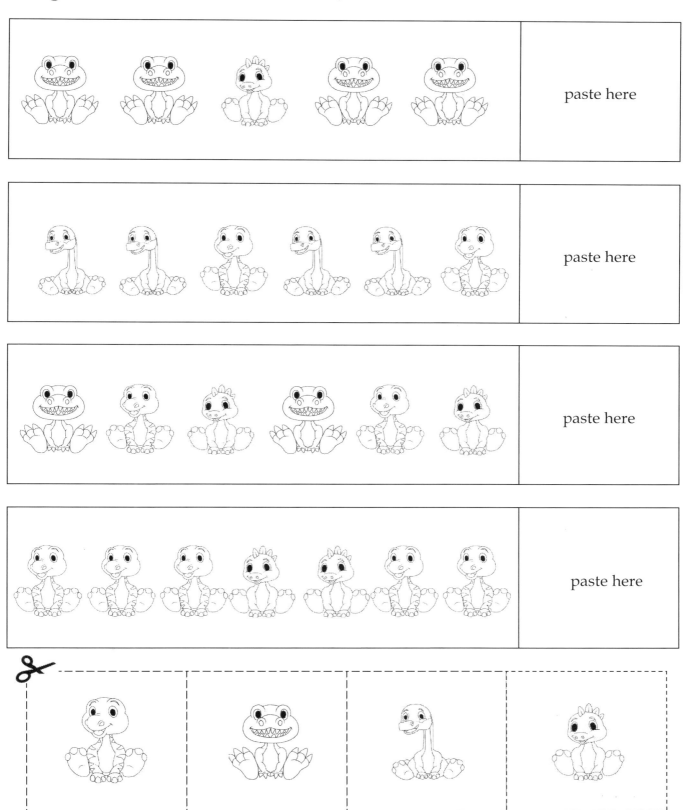

# The picture that comes next!

Look at the patterns below. Cut out the images and paste the image that comes last in each box.

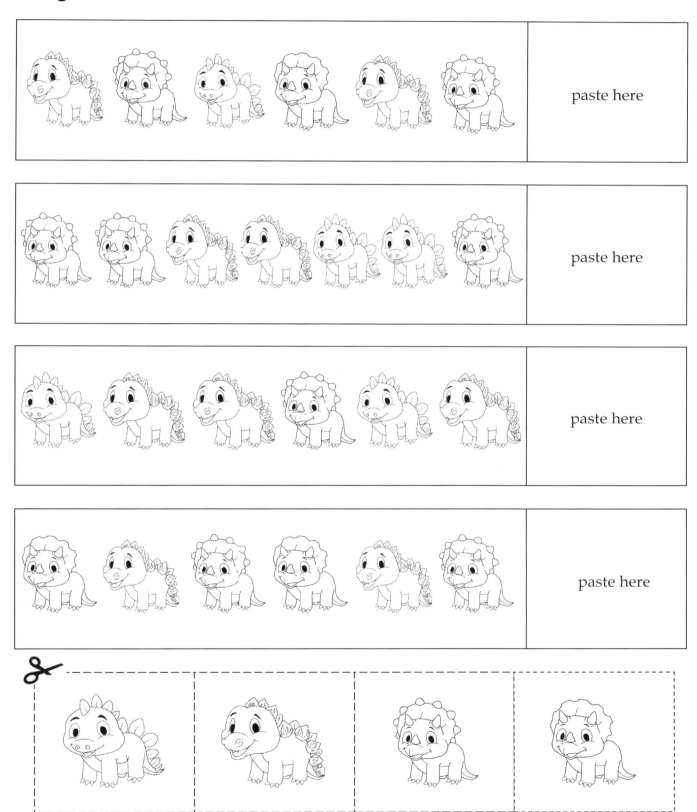

# Number Fun

Counting up from 1, which number comes next?

# Number Fun

Counting up from 1, which number comes next?

# Number Fun

Counting forward from **3**

Counting forward from **4**

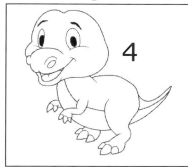

Counting forward from **1**

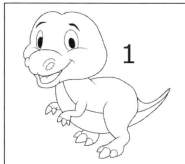

Counting forward from **7**

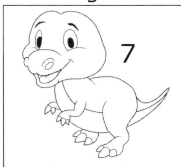

# Number Fun

Counting forward from **2**

Counting forward from **0**

Counting forward from **6**

Counting forward from **5**

# Number Fun

Find number in the pictures and compare, then color the one containing the **larger** number.

# Number Fun

Find number in the pictures and compare, then color the one containing the **larger** number.

# Number Fun

Find number in the pictures and compare, then color the one containing the **larger** number.

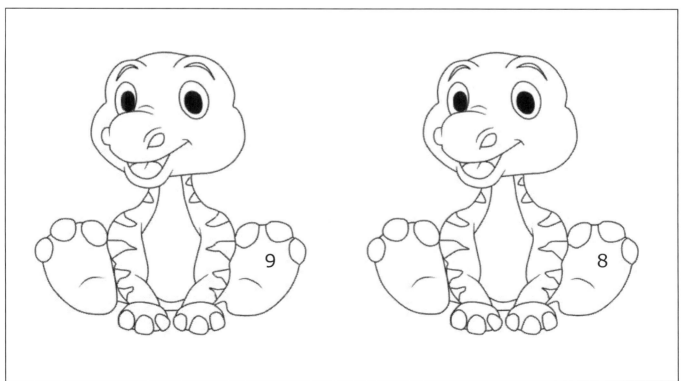

DATE: _____

TIME: _____

## Thank you!

Thank you for buying "Dinosaurs" Preschool Basics Activity Workbook we would be more than happy to consider how to apply your suggestion to the next edition. Without you voice, we can't exist.

**Please, support us and leave a review!**
We welcome your positive feedback and hope that others will benefit from your experience.